SPECTRUM®

Counting Money

Grade 2

Published by Spectrum®
an imprint of Carson-Dellosa Publishing
Greensboro, NC

Spectrum®
An imprint of Carson-Dellosa Publishing LLC
P.O. Box 35665
Greensboro, NC 27425 USA

ISBN 978-1-4838-3110-7

04-053217784

Table of Contents Counting Money

Lesson 1.2 Identifying and Counting Fives

A five-dollar bill is the same as .

You can write five dollars as **$5**.

Counting five-dollar bills is like skip counting by fives.

| 5 | 10 | 15 | 20 | 2 |

$25

Count the money. Write the missing numbers.

$_____ $10 $_____

$_____ $10 $_____ $_____ $_____ $_____

Count the money. Write how much in all.

 $_____

 $_____

 $_____

Lesson 1.3 Counting Ones and Fives

Count the money. Write the missing numbers.

Hint: Start counting by fives with the five-dollar bills.

Then, count on by ones with the one-dollar bills.

$5 $_____ $_____ $12

$5 $_____ $_____ $_____ $21 $_____ $_____ $_____

Count the money. Write how much in all.

$_____

$_____

$_____

Lesson 1.4 Solving Word Problems with Ones and Fives

SHOW YOUR WORK

Solve each problem.

Brad has 2 five-dollar bills.
His sister has 2 one-dollar bills.
How much money do they have?

$_____

Abby has 4 five-dollar bills in her wallet.
Her dad gives her 5 one-dollar bills
after she cleans her room.
How much money does Abby have now?

$_____

Zach has 15 five-dollar bills.
Grandma gives Zach 10 one-dollar bills
for his birthday.
How much money does Zach have now?

$_____

Anton has 8 five-dollar bills in his bank.
He gets 10 one-dollar bills from his
mom for walking the dog.
How much money does Anton have now?

$_____

Lesson 1.5 Identifying and Counting Tens

A ten-dollar bill  is the same as or

You can write ten dollars as **$10**.

Counting ten-dollar bills is like skip counting by tens.

| 10 | 20 | 30 | 40 | 50 | 60 | 70 |

$70

Count the money. Write the missing numbers.

$_____ $_____ $_____ $40 $_____

$_____ $_____ $30 $_____ $_____ $_____ $70 $_____ $_____

Count the money. Write how much in all.

 $_____

 $_____

 $_____

Lesson 1.6 Counting Ones, Fives, and Tens

Count the money. Write the missing numbers.

Hint: Start counting by tens with the ten-dollar bills.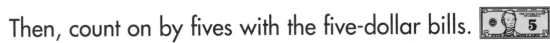

Then, count on by fives with the five-dollar bills.

Then, count on by ones with the one-dollar bills.

$____ $____ $____ $30 $____ $____

$____ $15 $____ $21 $____ $____

$____ $20 $____ $____ $36 $____

Count the money. Write how much in all.

$____

$____

$____

Lesson 1.7 Solving Word Problems with Ones, Fives, and Tens

SHOW YOUR WORK

Solve each problem.

Mark has 3 ten-dollar bills in his wallet.
He earns 3 five-dollar bills for raking.
How much money does Mark have now?

$_____

Rosie has saved 8 ten-dollar bills.
She earns 1 five-dollar bill and
3 one-dollar bills.
How much money does Rosie have now?

$_____

Freddy has 4 ten-dollar bills.
He earns 6 one-dollar bills for taking
the garbage out.
How much money does Freddy have?

$_____

Juan saves 3 ten-dollar bills.
Then, he saves 6 five-dollar bills.
Finally, he saves 15 one-dollar bills.
How much money does Juan save?

$_____

Check What You Learned

Counting Bills

Count the money. Write how much.

$_____

$_____

$_____

$_____

$_____

SHOW YOUR WORK

Solve the problem.

The family rakes leaves together.
Saul earns 1 ten-dollar bill.
Sofia earns 2 five-dollar bills.
Ralph earns 10 one-dollar bills.
How much money do they earn altogether?

$_____

NAME _____

 Check What You Know

Counting Coins

Count the money. Write the missing numbers.

_____¢   _____¢   3¢   _____¢

_____¢   2¢   _____¢   _____¢   _____¢   6¢   _____¢   _____¢

5¢   _____¢   _____¢   20¢   _____¢

_____¢   _____¢   _____¢   _____¢   50¢   _____¢

_____¢   _____¢   30¢   _____¢   _____¢   37¢   _____¢   _____¢

Count the money. Write how much in all.

           _____¢

               _____¢

Check What You Know

Counting Coins

Count the money. Write the missing numbers.

_____¢   50¢   _____¢   _____¢

_____¢   50¢   60¢   _____¢   _____¢   85¢   _____¢   _____¢

Count the money. Write how much in all.

_____¢

_____¢

SHOW YOUR WORK

Solve the problem.

Bella has 2 quarters, I dime, I nickel, and 2 pennies.

How much money does Bella have altogether?

$_____

Lesson 2.1 Identifying and Counting Pennies

A penny is **1¢**.

Counting pennies is similar to counting one-dollar bills.
Count by ones when you count pennies.

Count the money. Write the missing numbers.

_____¢   2¢   _____¢   _____¢

_____¢   _____¢

_____¢   _____¢   _____¢   4¢   _____¢   _____¢   7¢   _____¢

Count the money. Write how much in all.

          _____¢

      _____¢

   _____¢

     _____¢

       _____¢

Lesson 2.2 Identifying and Counting Nickels

A nickel is **5¢**.

Counting nickels is similar to counting five-dollar bills.
Count by fives when you count nickels.

Count the money. Write the missing numbers.

_____¢   10¢   _____¢   _____¢   _____¢

_____¢   10¢   _____¢   _____¢   _____¢   30¢   _____¢   _____¢

Count the money. Write how much in all.

         _____¢

            _____¢

      _____¢

         _____¢

           _____¢

Lesson 2.3 Counting Pennies and Nickels

Count the money. Write the missing numbers.

Hint: Start counting by fives with the nickels.

Then, count on by ones with the pennies.

_____¢   10¢   _____¢   _____¢   _____¢   14¢   _____¢

_____¢   _____¢   15¢   _____¢   _____¢   _____¢   27¢   _____¢

5¢   _____¢   _____¢   _____¢   17¢   _____¢   _____¢

Count the money. Write how much in all.

           _____¢

   _____¢

   _____¢

Lesson 2.4 Solving Word Problems with Pennies and Nickels

SHOW YOUR WORK

Solve each problem.

Sylvia has 2 nickels.
Amanda has 12 pennies.
How much money do they have?

_____ ¢

Denise has 2 nickels and 2 pennies.
Then, her mom gives her 1 more nickel.
How much money does Denise have now?

_____ ¢

Jordan has 3 nickels.
He finds 1 nickel and 7 pennies.
How much money does he have now?

_____ ¢

Mary buys a balloon for 3 nickels.
Then, she buys popcorn for 10 pennies.
How much money did Mary spend?

_____ ¢

Lesson 2.5 Identifying and Counting Dimes

A dime is **10¢**.

Counting dimes is similar to counting ten-dollar bills.
Count by tens when you count dimes.

Count the money. Write the missing numbers.

____¢ 20¢ ____¢ ____¢ ____¢ 60¢ ____¢

____¢ 20¢ ____¢ ____¢

____¢ ____¢ 30¢ ____¢ ____¢ ____¢ ____¢ 80¢ ____¢ ____¢

Count the money. Write how much in all.

    _____¢

       _____¢

  _____¢

      _____¢

          _____¢

Lesson 2.6 Counting Pennies, Nickels, and Dimes

Count the money. Write the missing numbers.

Hint: Start counting by tens with the dimes.

Then, count on by fives with the nickels.

Then, count on by ones with the pennies.

_____¢   20¢ _____¢ _____¢ _____¢ _____¢

_____¢   15¢ _____¢ _____¢ _____¢ _____¢ _____¢ _____¢

10¢ _____¢ _____¢ _____¢ 40¢ _____¢ _____¢ 43¢ _____¢

Count the money. Write how much in all.

       _____¢

          _____¢

            _____¢

Lesson 2.7 Solving Word Problems with Pennies, Nickels, and Dimes

SHOW YOUR WORK

Solve each problem.

Bonnie has 1 dime, 3 nickels, and
6 pennies. How much money does
she have?

_____ ¢

Ben has 2 dimes.
He finds 4 nickels and 5 pennies.
How much money does he have now?

_____ ¢

Liza buys milk for 2 dimes.
Noel buys carrots for 5 nickels.
Tracy buys popcorn for 10 pennies.
How much money do they spend?

_____ ¢

Tammy earns 5 dimes for washing dishes.
Then, she earns 3 nickels for making her bed.
Finally, she earns 15 pennies for walking
the dog.
How much money did Tammy earn?

_____ ¢

Lesson 2.8 Identifying and Counting Quarters

A quarter is **25¢**.

Counting quarters is like skip counting by twenty-fives.
There are 4 quarters in one dollar.

Count the money. Write the missing numbers.

_____¢   50¢

_____¢   _____¢   _____¢   100¢

_____¢

Count the money. Write how much in all.

     _____¢

    _____¢

      _____¢

   _____¢

Lesson 2.9 Counting Pennies, Nickels, Dimes, and Quarters

Count the money. Write the missing numbers.

Hint: Start counting by twenty-fives with the quarters.

Then, count by tens with the dimes.

Continue to count on by fives with the nickels.

Finally, count on by ones with the pennies.

_____¢   35¢   _____¢ _____¢ _____¢   65¢   _____¢ _____¢ _____¢

_____¢ _____¢ _____¢ _____¢ _____¢ _____¢   80¢   _____¢ _____¢

Count the money. Write how much in all.

 _____¢

 _____¢

 _____¢

 _____¢

Lesson 2.10 Solving Word Problems with Pennies, Nickels, Dimes, and Quarters

A pencil costs 1 quarter and 1 nickel.	A pen costs 1 quarter, 1 nickel, and 2 pennies.	A marker costs 4 dimes and 2 pennies.	A crayon costs 2 dimes and 4 pennies.

SHOW YOUR WORK

Use the chart to solve each problem.

Marco buys a pencil and a marker.
How much money does he spend? _____ ¢

Tam buys a pencil and a pen.
How much money does he spend? _____ ¢

Leah buys a pencil, a marker, and a crayon.
How much money does she spend? _____ ¢

Ada buys a pen and a crayon.
How much money does she spend? _____ ¢

Sylvie buys a marker and a crayon.
How much money does she spend? _____ ¢

Kato buys a pen, a crayon, and a pencil.
How much money does he spend? _____ ¢

Check What You Learned

Counting Coins

Count the money. Write the missing numbers.

_____¢ _____¢ _____¢ _____¢ _____¢ _____¢ _____¢ _____¢ _____¢

_____¢ _____¢ _____¢ _____¢ _____¢ _____¢ _____¢

Count the money. Write how much in all.

              _____¢

   _____¢

SHOW YOUR WORK

Solve each problem.

Colin has 2 quarters, 2 dimes, 3 nickels, and 3 pennies.
How much money does Colin have altogether?

_____¢

Laticia has 8 dimes, 2 nickels, and 9 pennies.
How much money does Laticia have altogether?

_____¢

Check What You Learned

Counting Coins

A banana costs 3 dimes and 1 nickel.	An apple costs 2 dimes.	An orange costs 3 dimes and 3 pennies.	A melon costs 2 quarters and 1 dime.

SHOW YOUR WORK

Use the chart to solve each problem.

Jada buys a melon and an apple.
How much money does she spend? _____ ¢

Devon buys a banana and an apple.
How much money does he spend? _____ ¢

Lexi buys a banana and a melon.
How much money does she spend? _____ ¢

Paul buys an orange, an apple, and a banana.
How much money does he spend? _____ ¢

Mid-Test Chapters 1–2

Count the money. Write the missing numbers.

$_____ $_____ $_____ $_____ $_____ $_____

$_____ $_____ $_____ $_____ $_____ $_____

$_____ $_____ $_____ $_____ $_____ $_____ $_____ $_____

Count the money. Write how much in all.

$_____

$_____

SHOW YOUR WORK

Solve the problem.

Sasha spends 2 five-dollar bills and
2 one-dollar bills on a new skirt.
Then, she spends 1 ten-dollar bill and
1 five-dollar bill on a shirt.
How much money does Sasha spend altogether?

$_____

Mid-Test Chapters 1–2

Count the money. Write the missing numbers.

____¢ ____¢ ____¢ ____¢ ____¢ ____¢ ____¢ ____¢ ____¢ ____¢ ____¢

Count the money. Write how much in all.

       _____¢

              _____¢

SHOW YOUR WORK

Solve each problem.

Victor spends 2 quarters, 2 nickels, and
3 pennies on a sandwich.
He spends 1 dime and 5 pennies on milk.
How much money does Victor spend
altogether?

_____¢

Tonya buys a book for 6 dimes and 3 nickels.
She buys a notebook for 1 quarter.
How much money does Tonya spend
altogether?

_____¢

CHAPTERS 1–2 MID-TEST

Check What You Know

Combining Coins

Count the money in each set of coins.

Write the amount. Then, answer the question.

 _____¢    _____¢

Are the sets of coins equal? _____

3 quarters	3 quarters
1 dime	2 dimes
2 nickels	5 pennies _____¢
2 pennies _____¢	

Are the sets of coins equal? _____

Circle the set of coins that equals the same amount as the first set.

Circle the list of coins that equals the same amount as the first list.

1 quarter	1 quarter	1 quarter	3 dimes
2 dimes	2 dimes	1 dime	5 nickels
4 nickels	1 nickel	5 nickels	6 pennies
3 pennies	8 pennies	8 pennies	

Check What You Know

Combining Coins

Circle the set of coins that equals 67¢.

Circle the coins that equal 73¢.	Circle the coins that equal 52¢.

Use the fewest possible coins to make 47¢. Tell how many coins of each kind you will use.	Use the fewest possible coins to make 66¢. Tell how many coins of each kind you will use.
_____ quarters	_____ quarters
_____ dimes 	_____ dimes
_____ nickels	_____ nickels
_____ pennies	_____ pennies

Lesson 3.1 Comparing Sets of Coins

Count the money in each set of coins.
Write the amount. Then, answer the question.

_____ ¢   _____ ¢

Are the sets of coins equal? _____

_____ ¢   _____ ¢

Are the sets of coins equal? _____

_____ ¢   _____ ¢

Are the sets of coins equal? _____

_____ ¢   _____ ¢

Are the sets of coins equal? _____

Lesson 3.2 Solving Word Problems for Comparing Sets of Coins

Count the amount of money described in each story.
Write the amount. Then, answer the question.

Finn found 1 dime, 1 nickel, and 4 pennies in his pocket on Sunday.	On Wednesday, Finn found 3 nickels and 4 pennies in his pocket.
_____¢	_____¢

Are the sets of coins equal? _____

Keisha had 1 quarter, 2 nickels, and 3 pennies to spend at the yard sale.	Toya had 1 quarter, 3 nickels, and 1 penny to spend at the yard sale.
_____¢	_____¢

Are the sets of coins equal? _____

Oliver bought nine lemon drops for 4 dimes and 1 nickel.	Oliver's brother Lucas bought 10 lemon drops for 3 dimes and 4 nickels.
_____¢	_____¢

Are the sets of coins equal? _____

Lesson 3.3 Making Equivalent Sets of Coins

Circle the coins that equal the same amount as the coins in the box.

Match the sets of coins that are equal.

A.    1.

B.    2.

C.    3.

D.    4.

Lesson 3.4 Solving Word Problems for Making Equivalent Sets of Coins

Each story describes an amount of money. Circle the list of coins below that equals the same amount.

To buy lemonade at Isaac's stand, you will need 1 quarter, 4 nickels, and 3 pennies.

1 quarter	4 dimes	4 dimes
2 dimes	1 nickel	2 nickels
1 nickel	3 pennies	8 pennies

Rashad had two trading cards that were the same. He sold the extra card to Trey for 3 quarters and 3 pennies.

1 quarter	5 dimes	4 dimes
4 dimes	5 nickels	3 nickels
2 nickels	5 pennies	8 pennies
3 pennies		

Each story describes an amount of money. In the space below, list a different set of coins that equals the same amount.

In her red purse, Kayla has 1 quarter, 4 nickels, and 9 pennies.

_____

The library had a book sale. Noah bought a book about space for 2 quarters, 1 dime, 1 nickel, and 10 pennies.

_____

Lesson 3.5 Making Sets of Coins to Fit a Total

Circle the set of coins that equals 44¢.

Circle the set of coins that equals 62¢.

Cross out the set of coins that does not equal 56¢.

Cross out the set of coins that does not equal 17¢.

Lesson 3.5 Making Sets of Coins to Fit a Total

Circle coins that equal 64¢.

Circle coins that equal 38¢.

Circle coins that equal 97¢.

Circle coins that equal 81¢.

Lesson 3.6 Making Sets with the Fewest Coins

Use the fewest possible coins to make each total.
Tell how many coins of each kind you will use.

72¢
__2__ quarters
__2__ dimes
__0__ nickels
__2__ pennies

67¢
_____ quarters
_____ dimes
_____ nickels
_____ pennies

48¢
_____ quarters
_____ dimes
_____ nickels
_____ pennies

55¢
_____ quarters
_____ dimes
_____ nickels
_____ pennies

83¢
_____ quarters
_____ dimes
_____ nickels
_____ pennies

27¢
_____ quarters
_____ dimes
_____ nickels
_____ pennies

92¢
_____ quarters
_____ dimes
_____ nickels
_____ pennies

39¢
_____ quarters
_____ dimes
_____ nickels
_____ pennies

Lesson 3.6 Making Sets with the Fewest Coins

Use the fewest possible coins to make 74¢. Tell how many coins of each kind you will use.

_____ quarters

_____ dimes

_____ nickels

_____ pennies

Now, create a different set of coins that equals 74¢. Tell how many coins of each kind you will use.

_____ quarters

_____ dimes

_____ nickels

_____ pennies

Use the fewest possible coins to make 63¢. Tell how many coins of each kind you will use.

_____ quarters

_____ dimes

_____ nickels

_____ pennies

Now, create a different set of coins that equals 63¢. Tell how many coins of each kind you will use.

_____ quarters

_____ dimes

_____ nickels

_____ pennies

Check What You Learned

Combining Coins

Count the money in each set of coins. Write the amount.
Then, answer the question.

 _____ ¢    _____ ¢

Are the sets of coins equal? _____

For each list of coins, write the amount. Below, describe
a different set of coins that equals the same amount.

2 dimes, 4 nickels,
4 pennies _____ ¢

1 quarter, 2 dimes,
3 nickels, 8 pennies _____ ¢

_____   _____

Use the fewest possible coins to
make 91¢. Tell how many coins
of each kind you will use.

_____ quarters

_____ dimes

_____ nickels

_____ pennies

Now, create a different set of
coins that equals 91¢. Tell how
many coins of each kind you
will use.

_____ quarters

_____ dimes

_____ nickels

_____ pennies

Check What You Know

Making Change

In each set, circle coins that equal $1.

Begin counting with the first coin shown. Then, count on to make a set of coins that equals $1. Circle the coins used.

Begin With	**Add to Make $1**

Count the coins. Tell how many more cents you need to make a group of 10. Then, draw more coins to equal $1. (Q 25) (N 5) (D 10) (P 1)

Begin With	**Add to Make a Group of Ten**	**Add to Make $1**
	_____ ¢	_____ ¢

Check What You Know

Making Change

Add the coins. Tell how many more of each coin you need to equal $1. Use the totals to complete the number sentence.

0 quarters, 3 dimes, 5 nickels, 8 pennies = _____ ¢

_____ quarters, _____ dimes, _____ nickels, _____ pennies = _____ ¢

_____ ¢ + _____ ¢ = $1

The first set of coins equals $1. Subtract the second set of coins. Complete the number sentence to show how much change is left.

1 quarter, 6 dimes, 2 nickels, 5 pennies = $1

0 quarters, 2 dimes, 1 nickel, 3 pennies = _____ ¢

$1 – _____ ¢ = _____ ¢

SHOW YOUR WORK

Solve each problem. Answer in cents and number of coins.

Ron has $1. He buys an apple for 21¢.

How much change does Ron have left? _____ ¢

_____ quarters, _____ dimes, _____ nickels, _____ pennies

Stew has $1. He buys a peach for 18¢.

How much change does Stew have left? _____ ¢

_____ quarters, _____ dimes, _____ nickels, _____ pennies

Lesson 4.1 Using Coins to Make $1

100 pennies = 100¢ = $1 	20 nickels = 100¢ = $1
10 dimes = 100¢ = $1	4 quarters = 100¢ = $1

Look at each set of coins. Circle coins to equal $1. Show four different ways to equal $1.

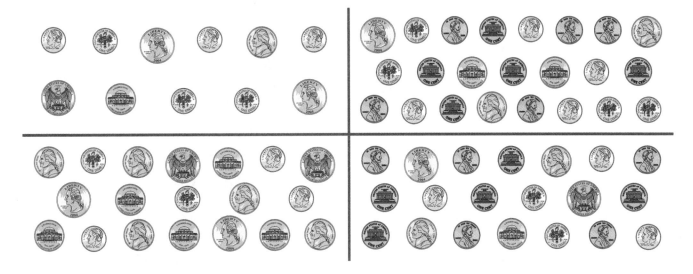

Make sets of coins to equal $1. Tell how many of each coin you need. Show four different ways to equal $1.

_____ quarters	_____ quarters	_____ quarters	_____ quarters
_____ dimes	_____ dimes	_____ dimes	_____ dimes
_____ nickels	_____ nickels	_____ nickels	_____ nickels
_____ pennies	_____ pennies	_____ pennies	_____ pennies

Lesson 4.1 Using Coins to Make $1

Begin counting with the first coin shown. Then, count on to make a set of coins that equals $1. Circle the coins used.

Begin With	Add to Make $1

Count the coins. Tell how many more cents you need to make a group of 10. Then, draw more coins to equal $1.

Begin With	Add to Make a Group of Ten	Add to Make $1
	2 ¢	Q Q D D D D
	_____ ¢	
	_____ ¢	

Spectrum Counting Money
Grade 2
46

Chapter 4, Lesson 1
Making Change

Lesson 4.1 Using Coins to Make $1

Add the first set of coins. Then, draw more coins to equal $1.
Complete the number sentence.

	(D) (D) (D) (D) (D) (P) (P)	
_48_ ¢	_52_ ¢	_48_ ¢ + _52_ ¢ = $1
_____ ¢	_____ ¢	_____ ¢ + _____ ¢ = $1
_____ ¢	_____ ¢	_____ ¢ + _____ ¢ = $1
_____ ¢	_____ ¢	_____ ¢ + _____ ¢ = $1
_____ ¢	_____ ¢	_____ ¢ + _____ ¢ = $1

Lesson 4.2 Solving Word Problems for Using Coins to Make $1

SHOW YOUR WORK

Write the amount described in each story. Then, tell how many more of each coin you need to equal $1. Check your work by completing the number sentence.

For raking leaves in the front yard,
Ian earned 1 quarter and 2 dimes. __45__¢

__1__ quarters, __2__ dimes, __2__ nickels, __0__ pennies = __55__¢

__45__¢ + __55__¢ = $1

Mario spent all his money
except 7 nickels and 8 pennies. _____¢

_____ quarters, _____ dimes, _____ nickels, _____ pennies = _____¢

_____¢ + _____¢ = $1

Nuria used a coupon to save
1 quarter, 1 nickel, and 5 pennies. _____¢

_____ quarters, _____ dimes, _____ nickels, _____ pennies = _____¢

_____¢ + _____¢ = $1

Lesson 4.2 Solving Word Problems for Using Coins to Make $1

SHOW YOUR WORK

Solve each problem.

Josh has 2 quarters, 1 dime, 5 nickels, and 2 pennies.

How much change does Josh have? _____¢

How much more change does Josh need to equal $1? _____¢

Mary Beth has 1 quarter, 1 dime, 3 nickels, and 8 pennies.

How much change does Mary Beth have? _____¢

How much more change does Mary Beth need to equal $1? _____¢

Max earns 2 quarters for feeding the dog.

He earns 3 dimes for cleaning the fish tank.

How much change does Max have? _____¢

How much more change does Max need to equal $1? _____¢

Tam finds 1 dime in his backpack, 3 nickels under his bed, and 7 pennies on his desk.

How much change does Tam have? _____¢

How much more change does Tam need to equal $1? _____¢

Anya has 1 quarter, 2 dimes, 1 nickel, and 6 pennies.

How much change does Anya have? _____¢

How much more change does Anya need to equal $1? _____¢

Lesson 4.3 Making Change from $1

Sasha has $1 to spend at each store. Circle the set of coins that shows the change she has after she buys each item. **Hint:** Count on from the cost of the item.

    =

$1

 +   =

$1

Fernando has $1 to spend at each store. Circle the set of coins that shows the change he has after he buys each item. **Hint:** Make a group of ten from the cost of the item and then count on.

 +   =

$1

 +   =

$1

Lesson 4.3 Making Change from $1

Philip has $1 to spend. Circle the set of coins that shows the change he has after he buys the item.

Now, check your work by adding his change to the cost of the item he buys.

_____ ¢ + [robot 63¢] = [$1]
                                $1

Maria has $1 to spend. Circle the set of coins that shows the change she has after she buys the item.

[$1] — [doll 46¢] = [coins]   [coins]
$1

Now, check your work by adding her change to the cost of the item she buys.

_____ ¢ + [doll 46¢] = [$1]
                                $1

Lesson 4.4 Solving Word Problems for Making Change from $1

SHOW YOUR WORK

Solve each problem. Draw coins if it helps you.

Josh has $1.

He buys an apple that costs 23¢.

How much change does Josh have left?

$1 – _____¢ = _____¢

Marcus has $1.

He buys a pen that costs 16¢.

How much change does Marcus have left?

$1 – _____¢ = _____¢

Caitlyn has $1.

She buys some flowers that cost 83¢.

How much change does Caitlyn have left?

$1 – _____¢ = _____¢

Kendra has $1.

She buys some strawberries that cost 79¢.

How much change does Kendra have left?

$1 – _____¢ = _____¢

Lesson 4.4 Solving Word Problems for Making Change from $1

SHOW YOUR WORK

 87¢   59¢   47¢   66¢

Solve each problem.

Aaron has $1. He buys a bag of marbles.

How much change does Aaron have left? __53__ ¢

How many of each coin does Aaron have left?

__2__ quarters, __0__ dimes, __0__ nickels, __3__ pennies

Rebecca has $1. She buys a book.

How much change does Rebecca have left? _____ ¢

How many of each coin does Rebecca have left?

_____ quarters, _____ dimes, _____ nickels, _____ pennies

Garrett has $1. He buys a baseball cap.

How much change does Garrett have left? _____ ¢

How many of each coin does Garrett have left?

_____ quarters, _____ dimes, _____ nickels, _____ pennies

Mike has $1. He buys a toy car.

How much change does Mike have left? _____ ¢

How many of each coin does Mike have left?

_____ quarters, _____ dimes, _____ nickels, _____ pennies

Check What You Learned

Making Change

Look at the set of coins. Circle coins to equal $1.

Make sets of coins to equal $1. Tell how many of each coin you need. Show two different ways to make $1.

_____ quarters, _____ dimes, _____ nickels, _____ pennies

_____ quarters, _____ dimes, _____ nickels, _____ pennies

Begin counting with the first coin shown. Then, count on to make a set of coins that equals $1. Circle the coins used.

Begin With | **Add to Make $1**

Count the coins. Tell how many more cents you need to make a group of 10. Then draw more coins to equal $1. (Q 25) (N 5) (D 10) (P 1)

Begin With | **Add to Make a Group of Ten** | **Add to Make $1**

_____ ¢ | _____ ¢

Check What You Learned

Making Change

Add the coins. Tell how many more of each coin you need to equal $1. Use the totals to complete the number sentence.

1 quarter, 2 dimes, 2 nickels, 9 pennies = _____¢

_____ quarters, _____ dimes, _____ nickels, _____ pennies = _____¢

_____¢ + _____¢ = $1

The first set of coins equals $1. Subtract the second set of coins. Complete the number sentence to show how much change is left.

0 quarters, 5 dimes, 9 nickels, 5 pennies = $1

0 quarters, 1 dime, 4 nickels, 2 pennies = _____¢

$1 – _____¢ = _____¢

SHOW YOUR WORK

Solve each problem. Answer in cents and number of coins.

Scott has $1. He buys a toy jet for 37¢.

How much change does Scott have left? _____¢

_2_ quarters, _____ dimes, _____ nickels, _____ pennies

Lara has $1. She buys a teddy bear for 24¢.

How much change does Lara have left? _____¢

_____ quarters, _____ dimes, _____ nickels, _____ pennies

Check What You Know

Adding and Subtracting Money

Add the dollars.

$23
+$ 6
$ _____

$34
+$14
$ _____

Subtract the dollars.

$ 9
−$ 3
$ _____

$15
−$ 5
$ _____

Add the cents.

15¢
+ 4¢
_____ ¢

19¢
+70¢
_____ ¢

Subtract the cents.

45¢
− 3¢
_____ ¢

85¢
−72¢
_____ ¢

SHOW YOUR WORK

Solve the problem using addition or subtraction.

Les has $27.

George has $41.

How much money do they have altogether? $ _____

Check What You Know

Adding and Subtracting Money

SHOW YOUR WORK

Solve each problem using addition or subtraction.

Malia has $68.
She buys a backpack for $24.
How much money does Malia have left? $_____

Jennifer has 13¢.
Clayton has 42¢.
How much money do they have altogether? _____¢

Nina has 89¢.
She buys a stamp for 49¢.
How much money does Nina have left? _____¢

Solve each problem.

Rachel buys a toy truck for $12 and a toy car for $6.		Javier has 25¢ to spend at the market. He buys an apple for 12¢.	
A toy truck costs	$	Javier has	¢
A toy car costs	+ $ ___	An apple costs	− ___ ¢
The two items cost	$	Javier has	¢ left

Lesson 5.1 Adding Dollars

Adding dollars is just like adding numbers. Add the money to find the total sum in dollars.

$\begin{array}{r} \$\ 9 \\ +\$\ 7 \\ \hline \$16 \end{array}$

$\begin{array}{r} \$13 \\ +\$12 \\ \hline \$ \end{array}$

$\begin{array}{r} \$\ 6 \\ +\$\ 5 \\ \hline \$ \end{array}$

$\begin{array}{r} \$17 \\ +\$22 \\ \hline \$ \end{array}$

$\begin{array}{r} \$\ 5 \\ +\$\ 8 \\ \hline \$ \end{array}$

$\begin{array}{r} \$36 \\ +\$22 \\ \hline \$ \end{array}$

$\begin{array}{r} \$12 \\ +\$46 \\ \hline \$ \end{array}$

$\begin{array}{r} \$15 \\ +\$\ 4 \\ \hline \$ \end{array}$

$\begin{array}{r} \$35 \\ +\$\ 5 \\ \hline \$ \end{array}$

$\begin{array}{r} \$15 \\ +\$\ 5 \\ \hline \$ \end{array}$

$\begin{array}{r} \$\ 8 \\ +\$\ 5 \\ \hline \$ \end{array}$

$\begin{array}{r} \$\ 9 \\ +\$\ 2 \\ \hline \$ \end{array}$

Lesson 5.2 Subtracting Dollars

Subtracting dollars is just like subtracting numbers. Subtract the money to find the difference in dollars.

$\begin{array}{r} \$\ 9 \\ -\$\ 7 \\ \hline \$\ 2 \end{array}$

$\begin{array}{r} \$57 \\ -\$36 \\ \hline \$ \end{array}$

$\begin{array}{r} \$49 \\ -\$\ 8 \\ \hline \$ \end{array}$

$\begin{array}{r} \$77 \\ -\$13 \\ \hline \$ \end{array}$

$\begin{array}{r} \$44 \\ -\$32 \\ \hline \$ \end{array}$

$\begin{array}{r} \$90 \\ -\$\ 7 \\ \hline \$ \end{array}$

Lesson 5.3 Adding and Subtracting Dollars

Add.

$15
+$ 4
$_____

$72
+$26
$_____

$61
+$38
$_____

Subtract.

$48
−$15
$_____

$76
−$30
$_____

$19
−$ 5
$_____

Lesson 5.4 Adding Cents

Adding cents is just like adding numbers. Add the money to find the total sum in cents.

$\begin{array}{r} 5¢ \\ + \ 3¢ \\ \hline ¢ \end{array}$	$\begin{array}{r} 57¢ \\ +41¢ \\ \hline ¢ \end{array}$
$\begin{array}{r} 17¢ \\ + \ 8¢ \\ \hline ¢ \end{array}$	$\begin{array}{r} 10¢ \\ + \ 9¢ \\ \hline ¢ \end{array}$
$\begin{array}{r} 13¢ \\ + \ 6¢ \\ \hline ¢ \end{array}$	$\begin{array}{r} 43¢ \\ +16¢ \\ \hline ¢ \end{array}$
$\begin{array}{r} 25¢ \\ +12¢ \\ \hline ¢ \end{array}$	$\begin{array}{r} 42¢ \\ +54¢ \\ \hline ¢ \end{array}$
$\begin{array}{r} 24¢ \\ + \ 5¢ \\ \hline ¢ \end{array}$	$\begin{array}{r} 19¢ \\ +60¢ \\ \hline ¢ \end{array}$
$\begin{array}{r} 55¢ \\ +30¢ \\ \hline ¢ \end{array}$	$\begin{array}{r} 34¢ \\ +36¢ \\ \hline ¢ \end{array}$

Lesson 5.5 Subtracting Cents

Subtracting cents is just like subtracting numbers. Subtract the money to find the difference in cents.

26¢
− 3¢
_____
¢

65¢
−61¢
_____
¢

17¢
− 9¢
_____
¢

88¢
−61¢
_____
¢

28¢
− 6¢
_____
¢

67¢
−12¢
_____
¢

67¢
−32¢
_____
¢

29¢
−12¢
_____
¢

35¢
−13¢
_____
¢

38¢
− 8¢
_____
¢

100¢
− 9¢
_____
¢

50¢
−26¢
_____
¢

Lesson 5.6 Adding and Subtracting Cents

Add.

15¢
+ 4¢
¢

14¢
+ 5¢
¢

36¢
+43¢
¢

61¢
+38¢
¢

74¢
+26¢
¢

80¢
+16¢
¢

Subtract.

16¢
– 8¢
¢

19¢
– 5¢
¢

56¢
–30¢
¢

78¢
–26¢
¢

60¢
–40¢
¢

49¢
–19¢
¢

Lesson 5.7 Solving Word Problems for Adding and Subtracting Dollars

Look at the items and how much they cost. Then, solve each problem.

 $23 $7 $12 $33 $4

Sammy plays baseball. He buys a baseball cap and a baseball.	Sasha has $20 to spend at the store. She buys a soccer ball.
A baseball cap costs $ 7	Sasha has $20
A baseball costs + $ _____	A soccer ball costs − $ _____
The two items cost $	Sasha has $ left
Tia practices her kicking skills. She buys a football and a soccer ball.	Raul has $45 to spend at the store. He buys a baseball bat.
	Raul has $
A football costs $	A baseball bat costs − $ _____
A soccer ball costs + $ _____	Raul has $ left
The two items cost $	
Sophie practices her throwing. She buys a baseball and a football.	Jay has $37 to spend at the store. He buys a football.
	Jay has $
A baseball costs $	A football costs − $ _____
A football costs + $ _____	Jay has $ left
The two items cost $	

Lesson 5.7 Solving Word Problems for Adding and Subtracting Dollars

SHOW YOUR WORK

Solve each problem using addition or subtraction.

Logan has $6.
He earns $9 more.
How much money does Logan have?

$_____

Abby has $22.
Anton has $34.
How much money do they have altogether?

$_____

Charlie earns $25 for walking the dog.
He earns $42 for shoveling snow.
How much money does Charlie earn?

$_____

Felix has $36.
He buys a pair of jeans for $22.
How much money does Felix have left?

$_____

Lesson 5.8 Solving Word Problems for Adding and Subtracting Cents

Look at the items and how much they cost. Then, solve each problem.

Emma buys a doll and a book.	Saul has 94¢ to spend at the store. He buys a toy truck.
A doll costs 5 6 ¢	Saul has 9 4 ¢
A book costs + _____ ¢	toy truck costs − _____ ¢
The two items cost _____ ¢	Saul has _____ ¢ left
Stuart buys a toy truck and a dinosaur.	Stacy has 29¢ to spend at the store. She buys a book.
A toy truck costs _____ ¢	Stacy has _____ ¢
A dinosaur costs + _____ ¢	book costs − _____ ¢
The two items cost _____ ¢	Stacy has _____ ¢ left
Pat buys a teddy bear. Tami buys a book.	Jaiden has 65¢ to spend at the store. She buys a teddy bear.
A teddy bear costs _____ ¢	Jaiden has _____ ¢
A book costs + _____ ¢	teddy bear costs − _____ ¢
The two items cost _____ ¢	Jaiden has _____ ¢ left

Lesson 5.8 Solving Word Problems for Adding and Subtracting Cents

SHOW YOUR WORK

Solve each problem using addition or subtraction.

Libby empties her piggy bank and counts 53¢.
After setting the table, she earns 25¢ more.
How much money does Libby have?

_____ ¢

Rahul has 73¢ in his pockets.
He finds 16¢ in the car.
How much money does Rahul have?

_____ ¢

Tony earns 20¢ for making his bed.
He earns 35¢ for cleaning his room.
How much money does Tony earn altogether?

_____ ¢

Kelly has 87¢.
She buys a smoothie for 50¢.
How much money does Kelly have left?

_____ ¢

Lesson 5.8 Solving Word Problems for Adding and Subtracting Cents

SHOW YOUR WORK

Solve each problem using addition or subtraction.

Dan finds 12¢ under his bed.
He finds 47¢ more in the couch.
How much money does Dan find altogether?

_____¢

Rita has 22¢.
She earns 55¢.
How much money does Rita have?

_____¢

Sarah has 14¢.
She gets 75¢ for folding laundry.
How much money does Sarah have?

_____¢

Miguel has 89¢.
He buys a sandwich for 44¢.
How much money does Miguel have left?

_____¢

Lesson 5.9 Solving Word Problems for Adding and Subtracting Dollars and Cents **SHOW YOUR WORK**

Read the story. Solve the problem using addition or subtraction.

Devon has $23 in the bank.
He gets $44 more for his birthday.
How much money does Devon have?

$_____

Roxy has 77¢.
She buys a necklace for 30¢.
How much money does Roxy have left?

_____¢

Megan earns 75¢ for feeding the cat.
She buys a muffin for 52¢.
How much money does Megan have left?

_____¢

Corey has $11.
Tina has $7.
How much money do they have altogether?

$_____

Lesson 5.9 Solving Word Problems for Adding and
Subtracting Dollars and Cents **SHOW YOUR WORK**

Look at the animals and how much they cost
at the pet shelter. Then, solve each problem.

Hope saves $69 for a dog.
She buys a dog at the shelter for $57.
How much money does Hope have left?

$_____

Kelsey buys a bird.
Juan buys a frog.
How much money do Kelsey and
Juan spend on pets altogether?

$_____

Liam buys a blue fish.
Then, he buys an orange fish.
How much money
does he spend on fish? _____¢

Next, Liam buys a snail.
How much money does
Liam spend altogether? _____¢

Check What You Learned

Adding and Subtracting Money

Add or subtract the dollars.

$$\begin{array}{r} \$51 \\ +\$37 \\ \hline \$ \end{array}$$

$$\begin{array}{r} \$72 \\ -\$11 \\ \hline \$ \end{array}$$

Add or subtract the cents.

$$\begin{array}{r} 6¢ \\ +\ 5¢ \\ \hline ¢ \end{array}$$

$$\begin{array}{r} 53¢ \\ +24¢ \\ \hline ¢ \end{array}$$

$$\begin{array}{r} 28¢ \\ -\ 6¢ \\ \hline ¢ \end{array}$$

$$\begin{array}{r} 67¢ \\ -24¢ \\ \hline ¢ \end{array}$$

SHOW YOUR WORK

Solve the problem using addition or subtraction.

Patty has $23.

Lou has $36.

How much money do they have altogether?

$_____

Check What You Learned

Adding and Subtracting Money

SHOW YOUR WORK

Solve each problem using addition or subtraction.

Elsa has $46.
She buys a scrapbook for $15.
How much money does Elsa have left? $_____

John has 63¢.
Clark has 31¢.
How much money do they have altogether? _____¢

Mackenzie has 74¢.
She buys a book for 30¢.
How much money does Mackenzie have left? _____¢

Solve each problem.

Kirsten buys a fancy hat for $42 and a baseball cap for $7.	Ryan has 78¢ to spend. He buys a highlighter for 46¢.
A fancy hat costs $	Ryan has ¢
A baseball cap costs + $ _____	A highlighter costs – _____ ¢
The two items cost $	Ryan has ¢ left

Final Test Chapters 1–5

Count the money. Write the missing numbers.

_____¢ _____¢ 45¢ _____¢ _____¢ _____¢ _____¢

Count the money. Write how much in all.

    $_____

SHOW YOUR WORK

Solve each problem.

Stan and Scott walk dogs for the neighbors.
Stan earns 2 ten-dollar bills.
Scott earns 3 five-dollar bills.
How much money do they earn altogether?

$_____

Lani has 4 dimes, 2 nickels, and 3 pennies.
How much money does Lani have altogether?

$_____

Final Test Chapters 1–5

Count the money in each set of coins. Write the amount.
Then, answer the question.

 _____ ¢ |  _____ ¢

Are these sets of coins equal? _____

Match the sets of coins that are equal.

A.    1.

B.    2.

C.    3.

Use the fewest possible coins to make 56¢. Tell how many coins of each kind you will use.	Now, create a different set of coins that equals 56¢. Tell how many coins of each kind you will use.
_____ quarters	_____ quarters
_____ dimes	_____ dimes
_____ nickels	_____ nickels
_____ pennies	_____ pennies

NAME _____

Final Test Chapters 1–5

Add the coins. Tell how many more of each coin you need to equal $1. Use the totals to complete the number sentence.

1 quarter, 3 dimes, 1 nickel, 8 pennies = _____¢

_____ quarters, _____ dimes, _____ nickels, _____ pennies = _____¢

_____¢ + _____¢ = $1

The first set of coins equals $1. Subtract the second set of coins. Complete the number sentence to show how much change is left.

1 quarter, 4 dimes, 5 nickels, 10 pennies = $1

0 quarters, 2 dimes, 1 nickel, 2 pennies = _____¢

$1 – _____¢ = _____¢

SHOW YOUR WORK

Solve each problem. Answer in cents and number of coins.

Troy has $1. He buys a teddy bear for 45¢.

How much change does Troy have left? _____¢

_____ quarters, _____ dimes, _____ nickels, _____ pennies

Vanessa has $1. She buys a book for 82¢.

How much change does Vanessa have left? _____¢

_____ quarters, _____ dimes, _____ nickels, _____ pennies

Final Test Chapters 1–5

Add or subtract the dollars.

$43
+$52
$

$65
−$22
$

Add or subtract the cents.

36¢
+51¢
___
¢

67¢
−16¢
___
¢

Solve each problem.

Gary buys a cowboy hat for $33 and a baseball cap for $13.	Edith has $38 to spend. She buys a fancy hat for $27.
The cowboy hat costs $	Edith has $
The baseball cap costs + $ _____	A fancy hat costs − $ _____
The two hats cost $	Edith has $ left
Chad buys a pen for 22¢ and a crayon for 14¢.	Kris has 88¢ to spend. She buys a highlighter for 33¢.
A pen costs ¢	Kris has ¢
A crayon costs + _____ ¢	A highlighter costs − _____ ¢
The two items cost ¢	Kris has ¢ left

Scoring Record for Posttests, Mid-Test, and Final Test

Chapter Posttest	Your Score	Performance			
		Excellent	Very Good	Fair	Needs Improvement
1	___ of 6	6	6	5	4 or fewer
2	___ of 24	24	22–23	17–21	16 or fewer
3	___ of 15	15	14	11–13	10 or fewer
4	___ of 33	33	30–32	23–29	22 or fewer
5	___ of 16	16	15	11–14	10 or fewer
Mid-Test	___ of 38	38	35–37	27–34	26 or fewer
Final Test	___ of 44	44	40–43	31–39	30 or fewer

Add up your correct answers on each test. For scoring purposes, count each blank as an answer. Then, record your test score in the Your Score column and see where your score falls in the Performance column. If your score is fair or needs improvement, review the chapter material again.

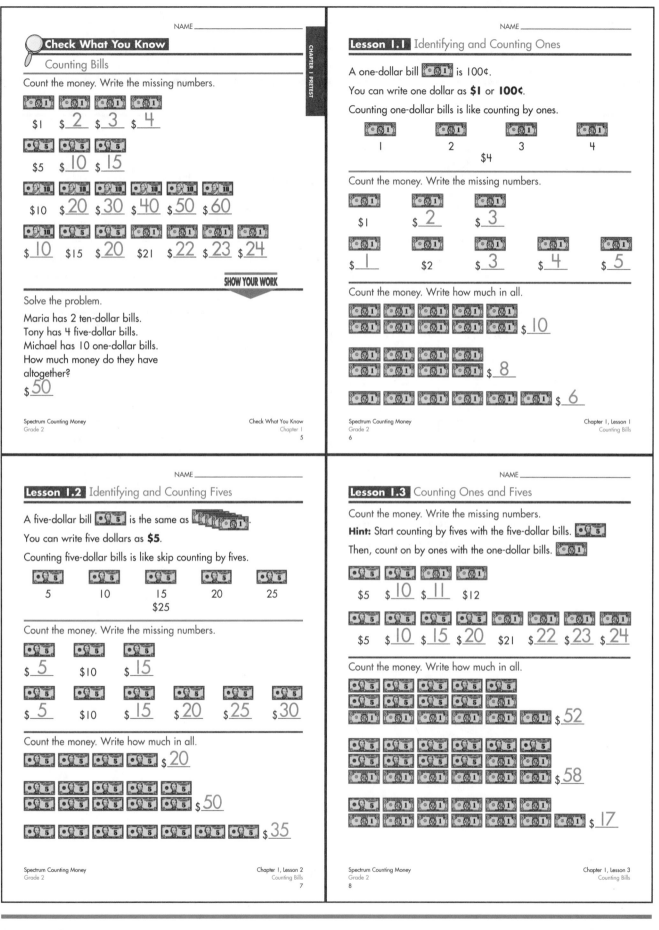

Check What You Know

Counting Bills

Count the money. Write the missing numbers.

$1 $ _2_ $ _3_ $ _4_

$5 $ _10_ $ _15_

$10 $ _20_ $ _30_ $ _40_ $ _50_ $ _60_

$ _10_ $15 $ _20_ $21 $ _22_ $ _23_ $ _24_

SHOW YOUR WORK

Solve the problem.

Maria has 2 ten-dollar bills.
Tony has 4 five-dollar bills.
Michael has 10 one-dollar bills.
How much money do they have altogether?

$ _50_

Lesson 1.1 Identifying and Counting Ones

A one-dollar bill is 100¢.

You can write one dollar as **$1** or **100¢**.

Counting one-dollar bills is like counting by ones.

1   2   3   4
         $4

Count the money. Write the missing numbers.

$1 $ _2_ $ _3_

$ _1_ $2 $ _3_ $ _4_ $ _5_

Count the money. Write how much in all.

$ _10_

$ _8_

$ _6_

Lesson 1.2 Identifying and Counting Fives

A five-dollar bill is the same as .

You can write five dollars as **$5**.

Counting five-dollar bills is like skip counting by fives.

5   10   15   20   25
              $25

Count the money. Write the missing numbers.

$ _5_ $10 $ _15_

$ _5_ $10 $ _15_ $ _20_ $ _25_ $ _30_

Count the money. Write how much in all.

$ _20_

$ _50_

$ _35_

Lesson 1.3 Counting Ones and Fives

Count the money. Write the missing numbers.

Hint: Start counting by fives with the five-dollar bills.

Then, count on by ones with the one-dollar bills.

$5 $ _10_ $ _11_ $12

$5 $ _10_ $ _15_ $ _20_ $21 $ _22_ $ _23_ $ _24_

Count the money. Write how much in all.

$ _52_

$ _58_

$ _17_

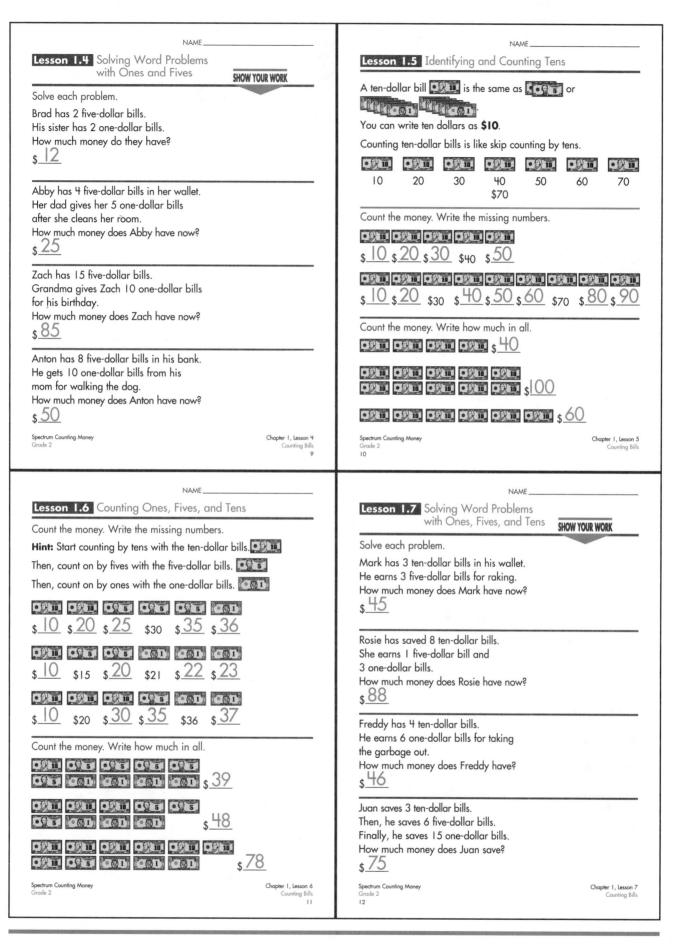

Lesson 1.4 Solving Word Problems with Ones and Fives

SHOW YOUR WORK

Solve each problem.

Brad has 2 five-dollar bills.
His sister has 2 one-dollar bills.
How much money do they have?

$ 12

Abby has 4 five-dollar bills in her wallet.
Her dad gives her 5 one-dollar bills
after she cleans her room.
How much money does Abby have now?

$ 25

Zach has 15 five-dollar bills.
Grandma gives Zach 10 one-dollar bills
for his birthday.
How much money does Zach have now?

$ 85

Anton has 8 five-dollar bills in his bank.
He gets 10 one-dollar bills from his
mom for walking the dog.
How much money does Anton have now?

$ 50

Lesson 1.5 Identifying and Counting Tens

A ten-dollar bill is the same as or .

You can write ten dollars as **$10**.

Counting ten-dollar bills is like skip counting by tens.

10 20 30 40 50 60 70
$70

Count the money. Write the missing numbers.

$ 10 $ 20 $ 30 $40 $ 50

$ 10 $ 20 $30 $ 40 $ 50 $ 60 $70 $ 80 $ 90

Count the money. Write how much in all.

$ 40

$ 100

$ 60

Lesson 1.6 Counting Ones, Fives, and Tens

Count the money. Write the missing numbers.

Hint: Start counting by tens with the ten-dollar bills.
Then, count on by fives with the five-dollar bills.
Then, count on by ones with the one-dollar bills.

$ 10 $ 20 $ 25 $30 $ 35 $ 36

$ 10 $15 $ 20 $21 $ 22 $ 23

$ 10 $20 $ 30 $ 35 $36 $ 37

Count the money. Write how much in all.

$ 39

$ 48

$ 78

Lesson 1.7 Solving Word Problems with Ones, Fives, and Tens

SHOW YOUR WORK

Solve each problem.

Mark has 3 ten-dollar bills in his wallet.
He earns 3 five-dollar bills for raking.
How much money does Mark have now?

$ 45

Rosie has saved 8 ten-dollar bills.
She earns 1 five-dollar bill and
3 one-dollar bills.
How much money does Rosie have now?

$ 88

Freddy has 4 ten-dollar bills.
He earns 6 one-dollar bills for taking
the garbage out.
How much money does Freddy have?

$ 46

Juan saves 3 ten-dollar bills.
Then, he saves 6 five-dollar bills.
Finally, he saves 15 one-dollar bills.
How much money does Juan save?

$ 75

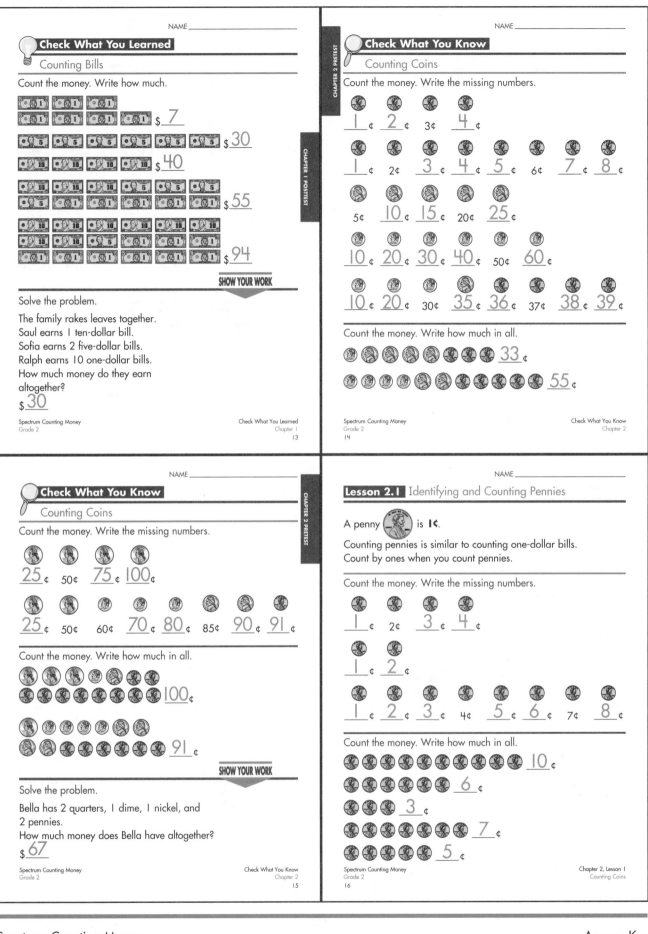

Answer Key

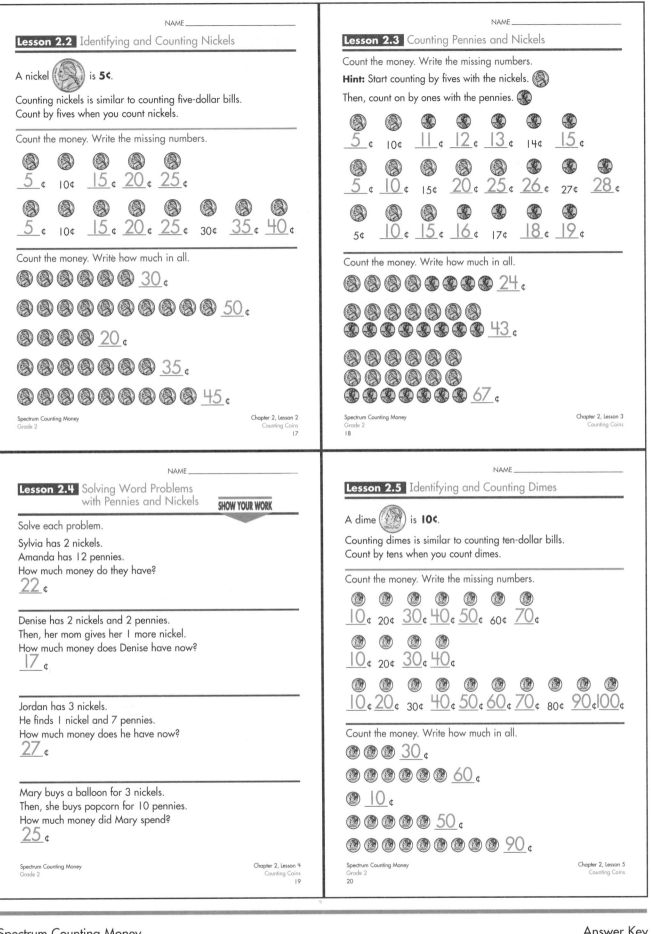

Lesson 2.2 Identifying and Counting Nickels

A nickel is **5¢**.

Counting nickels is similar to counting five-dollar bills.
Count by fives when you count nickels.

Count the money. Write the missing numbers.

_5_ ¢   10¢   _15_ ¢   _20_ ¢   _25_ ¢

_5_ ¢   10¢   _15_ ¢   _20_ ¢   _25_ ¢   30¢   _35_ ¢   _40_ ¢

Count the money. Write how much in all.

_30_ ¢

_50_ ¢

_20_ ¢

_35_ ¢

_45_ ¢

Spectrum Counting Money
Grade 2

Chapter 2, Lesson 2
Counting Coins
17

Lesson 2.3 Counting Pennies and Nickels

Count the money. Write the missing numbers.
Hint: Start counting by fives with the nickels.
Then, count on by ones with the pennies.

_5_ ¢   10¢   _11_ ¢   _12_ ¢   _13_ ¢   14¢   _15_ ¢

_5_ ¢   _10_ ¢   15¢   _20_ ¢   _25_ ¢   _26_ ¢   27¢   _28_ ¢

5¢   _10_ ¢   _15_ ¢   _16_ ¢   17¢   _18_ ¢   _19_ ¢

Count the money. Write how much in all.

_24_ ¢

_43_ ¢

_67_ ¢

Spectrum Counting Money
Grade 2
18

Chapter 2, Lesson 3
Counting Coins

Lesson 2.4 Solving Word Problems
with Pennies and Nickels

SHOW YOUR WORK

Solve each problem.

Sylvia has 2 nickels.
Amanda has 12 pennies.
How much money do they have?
_22_ ¢

Denise has 2 nickels and 2 pennies.
Then, her mom gives her 1 more nickel.
How much money does Denise have now?
_17_ ¢

Jordan has 3 nickels.
He finds 1 nickel and 7 pennies.
How much money does he have now?
_27_ ¢

Mary buys a balloon for 3 nickels.
Then, she buys popcorn for 10 pennies.
How much money did Mary spend?
_25_ ¢

Spectrum Counting Money
Grade 2

Chapter 2, Lesson 4
Counting Coins
19

Lesson 2.5 Identifying and Counting Dimes

A dime is **10¢**.

Counting dimes is similar to counting ten-dollar bills.
Count by tens when you count dimes.

Count the money. Write the missing numbers.

_10_ ¢   20¢   _30_ ¢   _40_ ¢   _50_ ¢   60¢   _70_ ¢

_10_ ¢   20¢   _30_ ¢   _40_ ¢

_10_ ¢   _20_ ¢   30¢   _40_ ¢   _50_ ¢   _60_ ¢   _70_ ¢   80¢   _90_ ¢   _100_ ¢

Count the money. Write how much in all.

_30_ ¢

_60_ ¢

_10_ ¢

_50_ ¢

_90_ ¢

Spectrum Counting Money
Grade 2
20

Chapter 2, Lesson 5
Counting Coins

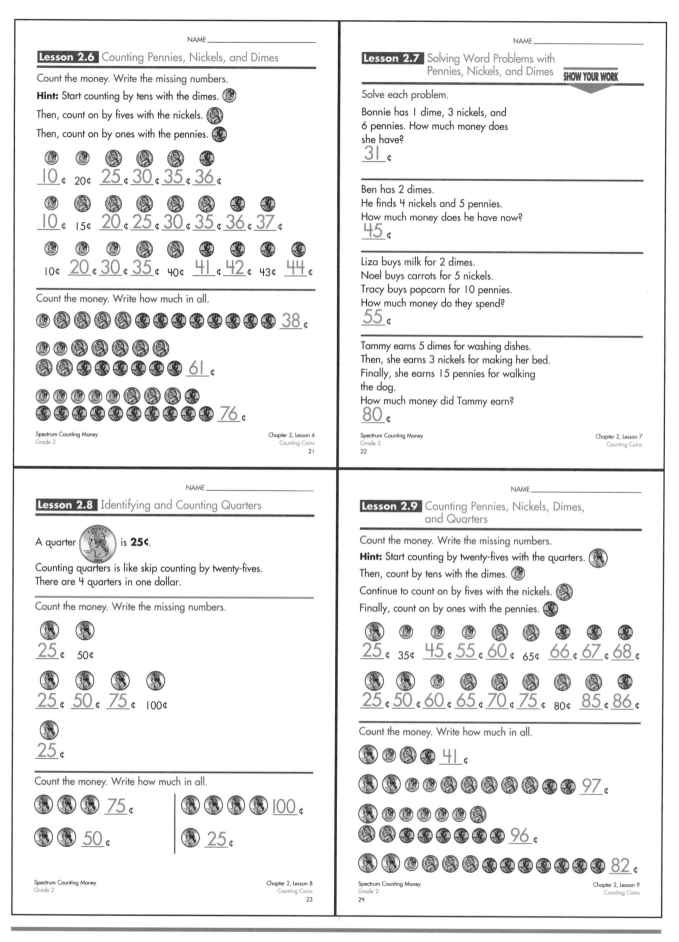

Lesson 2.6 Counting Pennies, Nickels, and Dimes

Count the money. Write the missing numbers.

Hint: Start counting by tens with the dimes.

Then, count on by fives with the nickels.

Then, count on by ones with the pennies.

10¢ 20¢ 25¢ 30¢ 35¢ 36¢

10¢ 15¢ 20¢ 25¢ 30¢ 35¢ 36¢ 37¢

10¢ 20¢ 30¢ 35¢ 40¢ 41¢ 42¢ 43¢ 44¢

Count the money. Write how much in all.

38¢

61¢

76¢

Lesson 2.7 Solving Word Problems with Pennies, Nickels, and Dimes

SHOW YOUR WORK

Solve each problem.

Bonnie has 1 dime, 3 nickels, and 6 pennies. How much money does she have?

31¢

Ben has 2 dimes.
He finds 4 nickels and 5 pennies.
How much money does he have now?

45¢

Liza buys milk for 2 dimes.
Noel buys carrots for 5 nickels.
Tracy buys popcorn for 10 pennies.
How much money do they spend?

55¢

Tammy earns 5 dimes for washing dishes.
Then, she earns 3 nickels for making her bed.
Finally, she earns 15 pennies for walking the dog.
How much money did Tammy earn?

80¢

Lesson 2.8 Identifying and Counting Quarters

A quarter is **25¢**.

Counting quarters is like skip counting by twenty-fives.
There are 4 quarters in one dollar.

Count the money. Write the missing numbers.

25¢ 50¢

25¢ 50¢ 75¢ 100¢

25¢

Count the money. Write how much in all.

75¢   100¢

50¢   25¢

Lesson 2.9 Counting Pennies, Nickels, Dimes, and Quarters

Count the money. Write the missing numbers.

Hint: Start counting by twenty-fives with the quarters.

Then, count by tens with the dimes.

Continue to count on by fives with the nickels.

Finally, count on by ones with the pennies.

25¢ 35¢ 45¢ 55¢ 60¢ 65¢ 66¢ 67¢ 68¢

25¢ 50¢ 60¢ 65¢ 70¢ 75¢ 80¢ 85¢ 86¢

Count the money. Write how much in all.

41¢

97¢

96¢

82¢

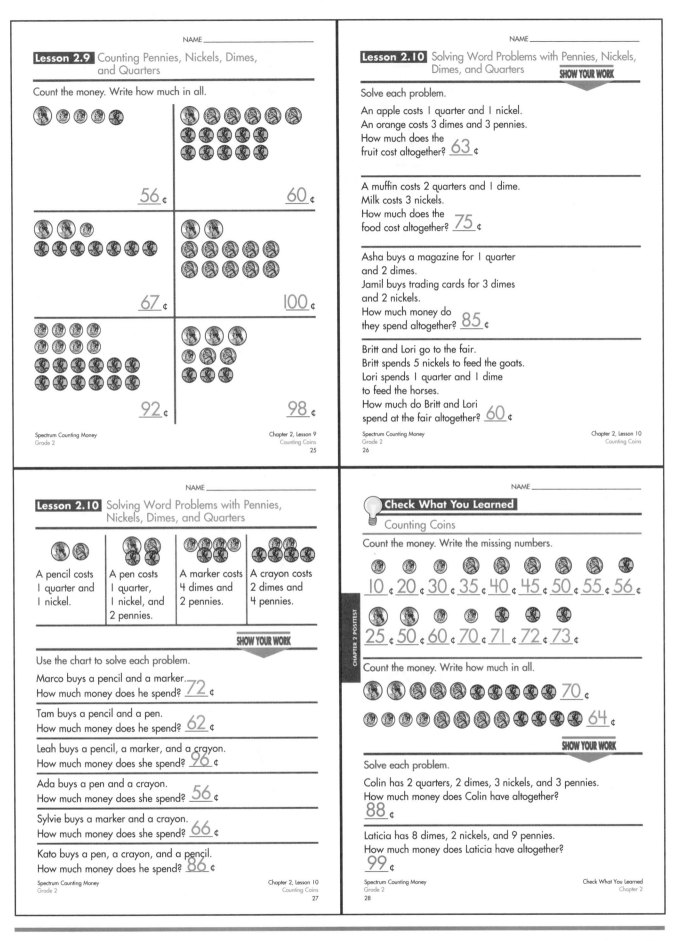

Lesson 2.9 Counting Pennies, Nickels, Dimes, and Quarters

Count the money. Write how much in all.

56 ¢   60 ¢

67 ¢   100 ¢

92 ¢   98 ¢

Lesson 2.10 Solving Word Problems with Pennies, Nickels, Dimes, and Quarters   **SHOW YOUR WORK**

Solve each problem.

An apple costs 1 quarter and 1 nickel.
An orange costs 3 dimes and 3 pennies.
How much does the
fruit cost altogether? 63 ¢

A muffin costs 2 quarters and 1 dime.
Milk costs 3 nickels.
How much does the
food cost altogether? 75 ¢

Asha buys a magazine for 1 quarter
and 2 dimes.
Jamil buys trading cards for 3 dimes
and 2 nickels.
How much money do
they spend altogether? 85 ¢

Britt and Lori go to the fair.
Britt spends 5 nickels to feed the goats.
Lori spends 1 quarter and 1 dime
to feed the horses.
How much do Britt and Lori
spend at the fair altogether? 60 ¢

Lesson 2.10 Solving Word Problems with Pennies, Nickels, Dimes, and Quarters

| A pencil costs 1 quarter and 1 nickel. | A pen costs 1 quarter, 1 nickel, and 2 pennies. | A marker costs 4 dimes and 2 pennies. | A crayon costs 2 dimes and 4 pennies. |

SHOW YOUR WORK

Use the chart to solve each problem.

Marco buys a pencil and a marker.
How much money does he spend? 72 ¢

Tam buys a pencil and a pen.
How much money does he spend? 62 ¢

Leah buys a pencil, a marker, and a crayon.
How much money does she spend? 96 ¢

Ada buys a pen and a crayon.
How much money does she spend? 56 ¢

Sylvie buys a marker and a crayon.
How much money does she spend? 66 ¢

Kato buys a pen, a crayon, and a pencil.
How much money does he spend? 86 ¢

Check What You Learned

Counting Coins

Count the money. Write the missing numbers.

10 ¢ 20 ¢ 30 ¢ 35 ¢ 40 ¢ 45 ¢ 50 ¢ 55 ¢ 56 ¢

25 ¢ 50 ¢ 60 ¢ 70 ¢ 71 ¢ 72 ¢ 73 ¢

Count the money. Write how much in all.

70 ¢

64 ¢

SHOW YOUR WORK

Solve each problem.

Colin has 2 quarters, 2 dimes, 3 nickels, and 3 pennies.
How much money does Colin have altogether?
88 ¢

Laticia has 8 dimes, 2 nickels, and 9 pennies.
How much money does Laticia have altogether?
99 ¢

CHAPTER 2 POSTTEST

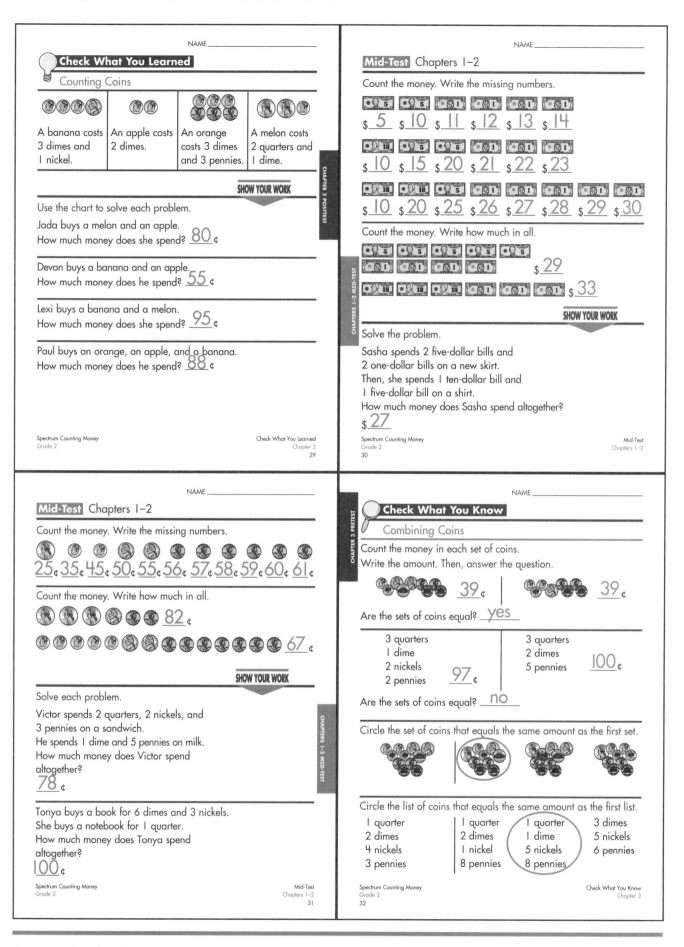

Answer Key

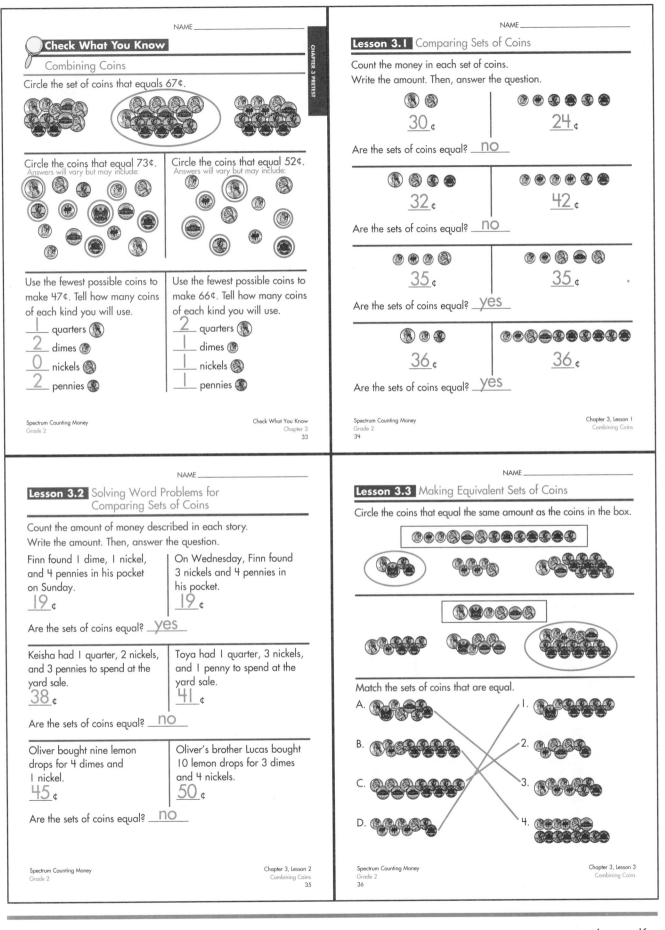

Check What You Know

Combining Coins

Circle the set of coins that equals 67¢.

Circle the coins that equal 73¢.
Answers will vary but may include:

Circle the coins that equal 52¢.
Answers will vary but may include:

Use the fewest possible coins to make 47¢. Tell how many coins of each kind you will use.

1 quarters
2 dimes
0 nickels
2 pennies

Use the fewest possible coins to make 66¢. Tell how many coins of each kind you will use.

2 quarters
1 dimes
1 nickels
1 pennies

Spectrum Counting Money
Grade 2

Check What You Know
Chapter 3
33

CHAPTER 3 PRETEST

Lesson 3.1 Comparing Sets of Coins

Count the money in each set of coins.
Write the amount. Then, answer the question.

30 ¢   24 ¢

Are the sets of coins equal? __no__

32 ¢   42 ¢

Are the sets of coins equal? __no__

35 ¢   35 ¢

Are the sets of coins equal? __yes__

36 ¢   36 ¢

Are the sets of coins equal? __yes__

Spectrum Counting Money
Grade 2
34

Chapter 3, Lesson 1
Combining Coins

Lesson 3.2 Solving Word Problems for Comparing Sets of Coins

Count the amount of money described in each story.
Write the amount. Then, answer the question.

Finn found 1 dime, 1 nickel, and 4 pennies in his pocket on Sunday.
19 ¢

On Wednesday, Finn found 3 nickels and 4 pennies in his pocket.
19 ¢

Are the sets of coins equal? __yes__

Keisha had 1 quarter, 2 nickels, and 3 pennies to spend at the yard sale.
38 ¢

Toya had 1 quarter, 3 nickels, and 1 penny to spend at the yard sale.
41 ¢

Are the sets of coins equal? __no__

Oliver bought nine lemon drops for 4 dimes and 1 nickel.
45 ¢

Oliver's brother Lucas bought 10 lemon drops for 3 dimes and 4 nickels.
50 ¢

Are the sets of coins equal? __no__

Spectrum Counting Money
Grade 2

Chapter 3, Lesson 2
Combining Coins
35

Lesson 3.3 Making Equivalent Sets of Coins

Circle the coins that equal the same amount as the coins in the box.

Match the sets of coins that are equal.

A.   1.

B.   2.

C.   3.

D.   4.

Spectrum Counting Money
Grade 2
36

Chapter 3, Lesson 3
Combining Coins

Lesson 3.4 Solving Word Problems for Making Equivalent Sets of Coins

Each story describes an amount of money. Circle the list of coins below that equals the same amount.

To buy lemonade at Isaac's stand, you will need 1 quarter, 4 nickels, and 3 pennies.

1 quarter	(4 dimes	4 dimes
2 dimes	1 nickel	2 nickels
1 nickel	3 pennies)	8 pennies

Rashad had two trading cards that were the same. He sold the extra card to Trey for 3 quarters and 3 pennies.

(1 quarter	5 dimes	4 dimes
4 dimes	5 nickels	3 nickels
2 nickels	5 pennies	8 pennies
3 pennies)		

Each story describes an amount of money. In the space below, list a different set of coins that equals the same amount.

In her red purse, Kayla has 1 quarter, 4 nickels, and 9 pennies.
Possible Answers: 2 dimes, 6 nickels, 4 pennies

The library had a book sale. Noah bought a book about space for 2 quarters, 1 dime, 1 nickel, and 10 pennies.
Possible Answers: 3 quarters

Lesson 3.5 Making Sets of Coins to Fit a Total

Circle the set of coins that equals 44¢.

Circle the set of coins that equals 62¢.

Cross out the set of coins that does not equal 56¢.

Cross out the set of coins that does not equal 17¢.

Lesson 3.5 Making Sets of Coins to Fit a Total

Circle coins that equal 64¢. Possible Answers:

Circle coins that equal 38¢. Possible Answers:

Circle coins that equal 97¢. Possible Answers:

Circle coins that equal 81¢. Possible Answers:

Lesson 3.6 Making Sets with the Fewest Coins

Use the fewest possible coins to make each total.
Tell how many coins of each kind you will use.

72¢	2 quarters	67¢	2 quarters
	2 dimes		1 dimes
	0 nickels		1 nickels
	2 pennies		2 pennies
48¢	1 quarters	55¢	2 quarters
	2 dimes		0 dimes
	0 nickels		1 nickels
	3 pennies		0 pennies
83¢	3 quarters	27¢	1 quarters
	0 dimes		0 dimes
	1 nickels		0 nickels
	3 pennies		2 pennies
92¢	3 quarters	39¢	1 quarters
	1 dimes		1 dimes
	1 nickels		0 nickels
	2 pennies		4 pennies

Lesson 3.6 Making Sets with the Fewest Coins

Use the fewest possible coins to make 74¢. Tell how many coins of each kind you will use.

<u>2</u> quarters
<u>2</u> dimes
<u>0</u> nickels
<u>4</u> pennies

Now, create a different set of coins that equals 74¢. Tell how many coins of each kind you will use. Possible Answers:

<u>0</u> quarters
<u>7</u> dimes
<u>0</u> nickels
<u>4</u> pennies

Use the fewest possible coins to make 63¢. Tell how many coins of each kind you will use.

<u>2</u> quarters
<u>1</u> dimes
<u>0</u> nickels
<u>3</u> pennies

Now, create a different set of coins that equals 63¢. Tell how many coins of each kind you will use. Possible Answers:

<u>0</u> quarters
<u>5</u> dimes
<u>2</u> nickels
<u>3</u> pennies

💡 Check What You Learned

Combining Coins

Count the money in each set of coins. Write the amount. Then, answer the question.

<u>72</u>¢ | <u>72</u>¢

Are the sets of coins equal? <u>yes</u>

For each list of coins, write the amount. Below, describe a different set of coins that equals the same amount.

2 dimes, 4 nickels, 4 pennies <u>44</u>¢

Possible Answers:
1 quarter, 1 dime, 9 pennies

1 quarter, 2 dimes, 3 nickels, 8 pennies <u>68</u>¢

Possible Answers:
2 quarters, 3 nickels, 3 pennies

Use the fewest possible coins to make 91¢. Tell how many coins of each kind you will use.

<u>3</u> quarters
<u>1</u> dimes
<u>1</u> nickels
<u>1</u> pennies

Now, create a different set of coins that equals 91¢. Tell how many coins of each kind you will use. Possible Answers:

<u>2</u> quarters
<u>4</u> dimes
<u>0</u> nickels
<u>1</u> pennies

🔍 Check What You Know

Making Change

In each set, circle coins that equal $1. Possible Answers:

Begin counting with the first coin shown. Then, count on to make a set of coins that equals $1. Circle the coins used. Possible Answers:

Begin With | **Add to Make $1**

Count the coins. Tell how many more cents you need to make a group of 10. Then, draw more coins to equal $1. (Q 25) (N 5) (D 10) (P 1)

Begin With	**Add to Make a Group of Ten**	**Add to Make $1**
	<u>1</u>¢	Possible Answers: Q Q Q D N <u>90</u>¢

🔍 Check What You Know

Making Change

Add the coins. Tell how many more of each coin you need to equal $1. Use the totals to complete the number sentence.

0 quarters, 3 dimes, 5 nickels, 8 pennies = <u>63</u>¢ Possible Answers:

<u>1</u> quarters, <u>0</u> dimes, <u>2</u> nickels, <u>2</u> pennies = <u>37</u>¢

<u>63</u>¢ + <u>37</u>¢ = $1

The first set of coins equals $1. Subtract the second set of coins. Complete the number sentence to show how much change is left.

1 quarter, 6 dimes, 2 nickels, 5 pennies = $1

0 quarters, 2 dimes, 1 nickel, 3 pennies = <u>28</u>¢

$1 – <u>28</u>¢ = <u>72</u>¢

▼ SHOW YOUR WORK

Solve each problem. Answer in cents and number of coins.

Ron has $1. He buys an apple for 21¢.
How much change does Ron have left? <u>79</u>¢

<u>3</u> quarters, <u>0</u> dimes, <u>0</u> nickels, <u>4</u> pennies

Stew has $1. He buys a peach for 18¢.
How much change does Stew have left? <u>82</u>¢ Possible Answers:

<u>3</u> quarters, <u>0</u> dimes, <u>1</u> nickels, <u>2</u> pennies

---

Lesson 4.1 Using Coins to Make $1

100 pennies = 100¢ = $1	20 nickels = 100¢ = $1
10 dimes = 100¢ = $1	4 quarters = 100¢ = $1

Look at each set of coins. Circle coins to equal $1. Show four different ways to equal $1. Possible Answers:

Make sets of coins to equal $1. Tell how many of each coin you need. Show four different ways to equal $1. Possible Answers:

1 quarters	2 quarters	3 quarters	0 quarters
2 dimes	1 dimes	0 dimes	5 dimes
1 nickels	8 nickels	4 nickels	6 nickels
50 pennies	0 pennies	5 pennies	20 pennies

Lesson 4.1 Using Coins to Make $1

Begin counting with the first coin shown. Then, count on to make a set of coins that equals $1. Circle the coins used. Possible Answers:

Begin With	Add to Make $1

Count the coins. Tell how many more cents you need to make a group of 10. Then, draw more coins to equal $1. Possible Answers:

Begin With	Add to Make a Group of Ten	Add to Make $1
	2 ¢	Q Q D D D D
	2 ¢	Q Q D
	1 ¢	Q Q Q D N

Lesson 4.1 Using Coins to Make $1

Add the first set of coins. Then, draw more coins to equal $1. Complete the number sentence. Possible Answers:

	D D D D D P P	
48 ¢	52 ¢	48 ¢ + 52 ¢ = $1
	Q D	
65 ¢	35 ¢	65 ¢ + 35 ¢ = $1
	D N N P P P P	
76 ¢	24 ¢	76 ¢ + 24 ¢ = $1
	Q D D	
55 ¢	45 ¢	55 ¢ + 45 ¢ = $1
	D P P P	
87 ¢	13 ¢	87 ¢ + 13 ¢ = $1

Lesson 4.2 Solving Word Problems for Using Coins to Make $1

SHOW YOUR WORK

Write the amount described in each story. Then, tell how many more of each coin you need to equal $1. Check your work by completing the number sentence.

For raking leaves in the front yard, Ian earned 1 quarter and 2 dimes. 45 ¢

1 quarters, 2 dimes, 2 nickels, 0 pennies = 55 ¢

45 ¢ + 55 ¢ = $1

Mario spent all his money except 7 nickels and 8 pennies. 43 ¢   Possible Answers:

0 quarters, 5 dimes, 1 nickels, 2 pennies = 57 ¢

43 ¢ + 57 ¢ = $1

Nuria used a coupon to save 1 quarter, 1 nickel, and 5 pennies. 35 ¢   Possible Answers:

2 quarters, 1 dimes, 1 nickels, 0 pennies = 65 ¢

35 ¢ + 65 ¢ = $1

Spectrum Counting Money

Grade 2

Answer Key

Lesson 4.2 Solving Word Problems for
Using Coins to Make $1

SHOW YOUR WORK

Solve each problem.

Josh has 2 quarters, 1 dime, 5 nickels, and 2 pennies.
How much change does Josh have? __87__ ¢
How much more change does Josh need to equal $1? __13__ ¢

Mary Beth has 1 quarter, 1 dime, 3 nickels, and 8 pennies.
How much change does Mary Beth have? __58__ ¢
How much more change does Mary Beth need to equal $1? __42__ ¢

Max earns 2 quarters for feeding the dog.
He earns 3 dimes for cleaning the fish tank.
How much change does Max have? __80__ ¢
How much more change does Max need to equal $1? __20__ ¢

Tam finds 1 dime in his backpack, 3 nickels under his bed,
and 7 pennies on his desk.
How much change does Tam have? __32__ ¢
How much more change does Tam need to equal $1? __68__ ¢

Anya has 1 quarter, 2 dimes, 1 nickel, and 6 pennies.
How much change does Anya have? __56__ ¢
How much more change does Anya need to equal $1? __44__ ¢

Lesson 4.3 Making Change from $1

Sasha has $1 to spend at each store. Circle the set of coins that
shows the change she has after she buys each item. **Hint:** Count
on from the cost of the item.

 +   = $1

 +   = $1

Fernando has $1 to spend at each store. Circle the set of coins
that shows the change he has after he buys each item. **Hint:** Make
a group of ten from the cost of the item and then count on.

 +   = $1

 +   = $1

Lesson 4.3 Making Change from $1

Philip has $1 to spend. Circle the set of coins that shows the
change he has after he buys the item.

 − =

Now, check your work by adding his change to the cost of the
item he buys.

__37__ ¢ + [robot] = $1

Maria has $1 to spend. Circle the set of coins that shows the
change she has after she buys the item.

$1 − =

Now, check your work by adding her change to the cost of the
item she buys.

__54__ ¢ + [toy] = $1

Lesson 4.4 Solving Word Problems for
Making Change from $1

SHOW YOUR WORK

Solve each problem. Draw coins if it helps you.

Josh has $1.
He buys an apple that costs 23¢.
How much change does Josh have left?
$1 − __23__ ¢ = __77__ ¢

Marcus has $1.
He buys a pen that costs 16¢.
How much change does Marcus have left?
$1 − __16__ ¢ = __84__ ¢

Caitlyn has $1.
She buys some flowers that cost 83¢.
How much change does Caitlyn have left?
$1 − __83__ ¢ = __17__ ¢

Kendra has $1.
She buys some strawberries that cost 79¢.
How much change does Kendra have left?
$1 − __79__ ¢ = __21__ ¢

Spectrum Counting Money

Grade 2

Answer Key

Lesson 4.4 Solving Word Problems for Making Change from $1

SHOW YOUR WORK

Solve each problem.

Aaron has $1. He buys a bag of marbles.

How much change does Aaron have left? __53__ ¢

How many of each coin does Aaron have left?

__2__ quarters, __0__ dimes, __0__ nickels, __3__ pennies

Rebecca has $1. She buys a book.

How much change does Rebecca have left? __34__ ¢

How many of each coin does Rebecca have left? Possible Answers:

__0__ quarters, __3__ dimes, __0__ nickels, __4__ pennies

Garrett has $1. He buys a baseball cap.

How much change does Garrett have left? __13__ ¢

How many of each coin does Garrett have left? Possible Answers:

__0__ quarters, __1__ dimes, __0__ nickels, __3__ pennies

Mike has $1. He buys a toy car.

How much change does Mike have left? __41__ ¢

How many of each coin does Mike have left? Possible Answers:

__1__ quarters, __1__ dimes, __1__ nickels, __1__ pennies

Spectrum Counting Money
Grade 2

Chapter 4, Lesson 4
Making Change
53

Check What You Learned

Making Change

CHAPTER 4 POSTTEST

Look at the set of coins. Circle coins to equal $1. Possible Answers:

Make sets of coins to equal $1. Tell how many of each coin you need. Show two different ways to make $1. Possible Answers:

__1__ quarters, __3__ dimes, __7__ nickels, __10__ pennies
__2__ quarters, __3__ dimes, __2__ nickels, __10__ pennies

Begin counting with the first coin shown. Then, count on to make a set of coins that equals $1. Circle the coins used.

Begin With | **Add to Make $1**

Count the coins. Tell how many more cents you need to make a group of 10. Then draw more coins to equal $1. (Q 25) (N 5) (D 10) (P 1)

Begin With | **Add to Make a Group of Ten** | **Add to Make $1**
 | | Possible Answers:
 | __2__ ¢ | (Q)(D)(D)(N)(N)(N)(N) __70__ ¢

Spectrum Counting Money
Grade 2

Check What You Learned
Chapter 4
54

Check What You Learned

Making Change

Add the coins. Tell how many more of each coin you need to equal $1. Use the totals to complete the number sentence.

1 quarter, 2 dimes, 2 nickels, 9 pennies = __64__ ¢ Possible Answers:

__1__ quarters, __0__ dimes, __2__ nickels, __1__ pennies = __36__ ¢

__64__ ¢ + __36__ ¢ = $1

CHAPTER 4 POSTTEST

The first set of coins equals $1. Subtract the second set of coins. Complete the number sentence to show how much change is left.

0 quarters, 5 dimes, 9 nickels, 5 pennies = $1

0 quarters, 1 dime, 4 nickels, 2 pennies = __32__ ¢

$1 – __32__ ¢ = __68__ ¢

SHOW YOUR WORK

Solve each problem. Answer in cents and number of coins.

Scott has $1. He buys a toy jet for 37¢.

How much change does Scott have left? __63__ ¢ Possible Answers:

__2__ quarters, __1__ dimes, __0__ nickels, __3__ pennies

Lara has $1. She buys a teddy bear for 24¢.

How much change does Lara have left? __76__ ¢ Possible Answers:

__2__ quarters, __2__ dimes, __1__ nickels, __1__ pennies

Spectrum Counting Money
Grade 2

Check What You Learned
Chapter 4
55

Check What You Know

CHAPTER 5 PRETEST

Adding and Subtracting Money

Add the dollars.

$23 | $34
+$ 6 | +$14
$29 | $48

Subtract the dollars.

$ 9 | $15
–$ 3 | –$ 5
$ 6 | $10

Add the cents.

15¢ | 19¢
+ 4¢ | +70¢
19 ¢ | 89 ¢

Subtract the cents.

45¢ | 85¢
– 3¢ | –72¢
42 ¢ | 13 ¢

SHOW YOUR WORK

Solve the problem using addition or subtraction.

Les has $27.

George has $41.

How much money do they have altogether? $__68__

Spectrum Counting Money
Grade 2

Check What You Know
Chapter 5
56

Spectrum Counting Money

Grade 2

90

Answer Key

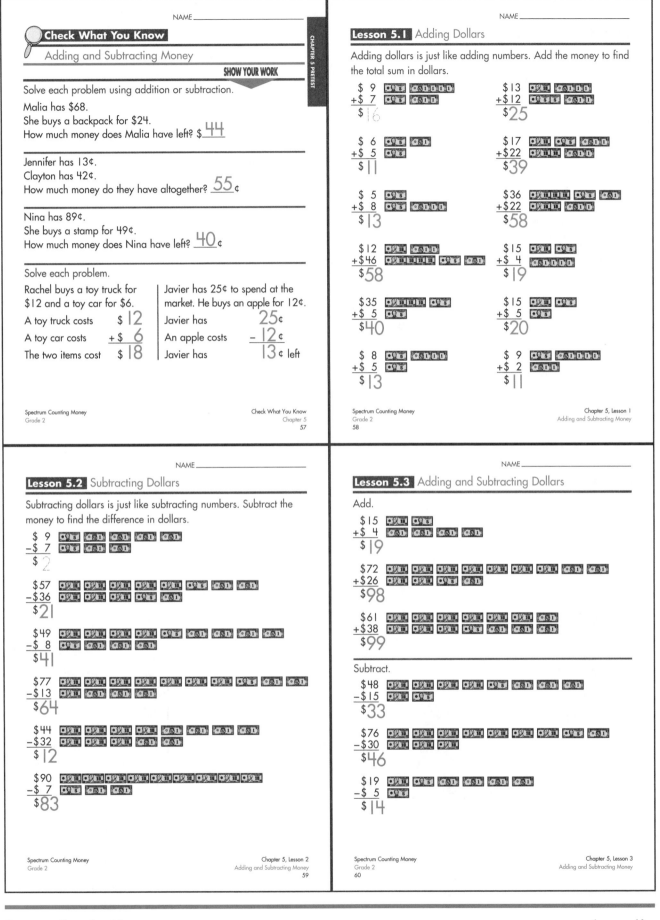

Check What You Know

Adding and Subtracting Money

CHAPTER 5 PRETEST

SHOW YOUR WORK

Solve each problem using addition or subtraction.

Malia has $68.
She buys a backpack for $24.
How much money does Malia have left? $ 44

Jennifer has 13¢.
Clayton has 42¢.
How much money do they have altogether? 55 ¢

Nina has 89¢.
She buys a stamp for 49¢.
How much money does Nina have left? 40 ¢

Solve each problem.

Rachel buys a toy truck for $12 and a toy car for $6.

A toy truck costs $ 12
A toy car costs   +$ 6
The two items cost $ 18

Javier has 25¢ to spend at the market. He buys an apple for 12¢.

Javier has   25¢
An apple costs   – 12 ¢
Javier has   13 ¢ left

Spectrum Counting Money
Grade 2

Check What You Know
Chapter 5
57

Lesson 5.1 Adding Dollars

Adding dollars is just like adding numbers. Add the money to find the total sum in dollars.

$ 9
+$ 7
$ 16

$13
+$12
$25

$ 6
+$ 5
$ 11

$17
+$22
$39

$ 5
+$ 8
$ 13

$36
+$22
$58

$12
+$46
$58

$15
+$ 4
$ 19

$35
+$ 5
$40

$15
+$ 5
$20

$ 8
+$ 5
$ 13

$ 9
+$ 2
$ 11

Spectrum Counting Money
Grade 2
58

Chapter 5, Lesson 1
Adding and Subtracting Money

Lesson 5.2 Subtracting Dollars

Subtracting dollars is just like subtracting numbers. Subtract the money to find the difference in dollars.

$ 9
–$ 7
$ 2

$57
–$36
$21

$49
–$ 8
$41

$77
–$13
$64

$44
–$32
$12

$90
–$ 7
$83

Spectrum Counting Money
Grade 2

Chapter 5, Lesson 2
Adding and Subtracting Money
59

Lesson 5.3 Adding and Subtracting Dollars

Add.

$15
+$ 4
$19

$72
+$26
$98

$61
+$38
$99

Subtract.

$48
–$15
$33

$76
–$30
$46

$19
–$ 5
$14

Spectrum Counting Money
Grade 2
60

Chapter 5, Lesson 3
Adding and Subtracting Money

Spectrum Counting Money
Grade 2

Answer Key

Lesson 5.4 Adding Cents

Adding cents is just like adding numbers. Add the money to find the total sum in cents.

5¢ + 3¢ **8¢**	57¢ +41¢ **98¢**
17¢ + 8¢ **25¢**	10¢ + 9¢ **19¢**
13¢ + 6¢ **19¢**	43¢ +16¢ **59¢**
25¢ +12¢ **37¢**	42¢ +54¢ **96¢**
24¢ + 5¢ **29¢**	19¢ +60¢ **79¢**
55¢ +30¢ **85¢**	34¢ +36¢ **70¢**

Lesson 5.5 Subtracting Cents

Subtracting cents is just like subtracting numbers. Subtract the money to find the difference in cents.

26¢ − 3¢ **23¢**	65¢ −61¢ **4¢**
17¢ − 9¢ **8¢**	88¢ −61¢ **27¢**
28¢ − 6¢ **22¢**	67¢ −12¢ **55¢**
67¢ −32¢ **35¢**	29¢ −12¢ **17¢**
35¢ −13¢ **22¢**	38¢ − 8¢ **30¢**
100¢ − 9¢ **91¢**	50¢ −26¢ **24¢**

Lesson 5.6 Adding and Subtracting Cents

Add.

15¢ + 4¢ **19¢**	14¢ + 5¢ **19¢**
36¢ +43¢ **79¢**	61¢ +38¢ **99¢**
74¢ +26¢ **100¢**	80¢ +16¢ **96¢**

Subtract.

16¢ − 8¢ **8¢**	19¢ − 5¢ **14¢**
56¢ −30¢ **26¢**	78¢ −26¢ **52¢**
60¢ −40¢ **20¢**	49¢ −19¢ **30¢**

Lesson 5.7 Solving Word Problems for Adding and Subtracting Dollars

Look at the items and how much they cost. Then, solve each problem.

Sammy plays baseball. He buys a baseball cap and a baseball. A baseball cap costs $ **7** A baseball costs + $ **4** The two items cost $ **11**	Sasha has $20 to spend at the store. She buys a soccer ball. Sasha has $ **20** A soccer ball costs − $ **12** Sasha has $ **8** left
Tia practices her kicking skills. She buys a football and a soccer ball. A football costs $ **23** A soccer ball costs + $ **12** The two items cost $ **35**	Raul has $45 to spend at the store. He buys a baseball bat. Raul has $ **45** A baseball bat costs − $ **33** Raul has $ **12** left
Sophie practices her throwing. She buys a baseball and a football. A baseball costs $ **4** A football costs + $ **23** The two items cost $ **27**	Jay has $37 to spend at the store. He buys a football. Jay has $ **37** A football costs − $ **23** Jay has $ **14** left

---

Lesson 5.7 Solving Word Problems for Adding
and Subtracting Dollars **SHOW YOUR WORK**

Solve each problem using addition or subtraction.

Logan has $6.
He earns $9 more.
How much money does Logan have?

$ 15

Abby has $22.
Anton has $34.
How much money do they have altogether?

$ 56

Charlie earns $25 for walking the dog.
He earns $42 for shoveling snow.
How much money does Charlie earn?

$ 67

Felix has $36.
He buys a pair of jeans for $22.
How much money does Felix have left?

$ 14

Lesson 5.8 Solving Word Problems for Adding
and Subtracting Cents

Look at the items and how much they cost. Then, solve each problem.

Emma buys a doll and a book.		Saul has 94¢ to spend at the store. He buys a toy truck.		
A doll costs	56¢	Saul has	94¢	
A book costs	+ 12¢	toy truck costs	− 74¢	
The two items cost	68¢	Saul has	20¢ left	
Stuart buys a toy truck and a dinosaur.		Stacy has 29¢ to spend at the store. She buys a book.		
A toy truck costs	74¢	Stacy has	29¢	
A dinosaur costs	+ 22¢	book costs	− 12¢	
The two items cost	96¢	Stacy has	17¢ left	
Pat buys a teddy bear. Tami buys a book.		Jaiden has 65¢ to spend at the store. She buys a teddy bear.		
A teddy bear costs	43¢	Jaiden has	65¢	
A book costs	+ 12¢	teddy bear costs	− 43¢	
The two items cost	55¢	Jaiden has	22¢ left	

Lesson 5.8 Solving Word Problems for Adding
and Subtracting Cents **SHOW YOUR WORK**

Solve each problem using addition or subtraction.

Libby empties her piggy bank and counts 53¢.
After setting the table, she earns 25¢ more.
How much money does Libby have?

78 ¢

Rahul has 73¢ in his pockets.
He finds 16¢ in the car.
How much money does Rahul have?

89 ¢

Tony earns 20¢ for making his bed.
He earns 35¢ for cleaning his room.
How much money does Tony earn altogether?

55 ¢

Kelly has 87¢.
She buys a smoothie for 50¢.
How much money does Kelly have left?

37 ¢

Lesson 5.8 Solving Word Problems for Adding
and Subtracting Cents **SHOW YOUR WORK**

Solve each problem using addition or subtraction.

Dan finds 12¢ under his bed.
He finds 47¢ more in the couch.
How much money does Dan find altogether?

59 ¢

Rita has 22¢.
She earns 55¢.
How much money does Rita have?

77 ¢

Sarah has 14¢.
She gets 75¢ for folding laundry.
How much money does Sarah have?

89 ¢

Miguel has 89¢.
He buys a sandwich for 44¢.
How much money does Miguel have left?

45 ¢

Lesson 5.9 Solving Word Problems for Adding and
Subtracting Dollars and Cents **SHOW YOUR WORK**

Read the story. Solve the problem using addition
or subtraction.

Devon has $23 in the bank.
He gets $44 more for his birthday.
How much money does Devon have?
$ _67_

Roxy has 77¢.
She buys a necklace for 30¢.
How much money does Roxy have left?
_47_ ¢

Megan earns 75¢ for feeding the cat.
She buys a muffin for 52¢.
How much money does Megan have left?
_23_ ¢

Corey has $11.
Tina has $7.
How much money do they have altogether?
$ _18_

Lesson 5.9 Solving Word Problems for Adding and
Subtracting Dollars and Cents **SHOW YOUR WORK**

Look at the animals and how much they cost
at the pet shelter. Then, solve each problem.

Hope saves $69 for a dog.
She buys a dog at the shelter for $57.
How much money does Hope have left?
$ _12_

Kelsey buys a bird.
Juan buys a frog.
How much money do Kelsey and
Juan spend on pets altogether?
$ _25_

Liam buys a blue fish.
Then, he buys an orange fish.
How much money
does he spend on fish? _85_ ¢

Next, Liam buys a snail.
How much money does
Liam spend altogether? _95_ ¢

💡 **Check What You Learned**

Adding and Subtracting Money

Add or subtract the dollars.

$51
+$37
$88

$72
−$11
$61

Add or subtract the cents.

6¢
+ 5¢
11¢

53¢
+24¢
77¢

28¢
− 6¢
22¢

67¢
−24¢
43¢

SHOW YOUR WORK

Solve the problem using addition or subtraction.

Patty has $23.
Lou has $36.
How much money do they have altogether?
$ _59_

💡 **Check What You Learned**

Adding and Subtracting Money

SHOW YOUR WORK

Solve each problem using addition or subtraction.

Elsa has $46.
She buys a scrapbook for $15.
How much money does Elsa have left? $ _31_

John has 63¢.
Clark has 31¢.
How much money do they have altogether? _94_ ¢

Mackenzie has 74¢.
She buys a book for 30¢.
How much money does Mackenzie have left? _44_ ¢

Solve each problem.

Kirsten buys a fancy hat for $42 and a baseball cap for $7.	Ryan has 78¢ to spend. He buys a highlighter for 46¢.
A fancy hat costs $42	Ryan has 78¢
A baseball cap costs + $ 7	A highlighter costs − 46¢
The two items cost $49	Ryan has 32¢ left

CHAPTER 5 POSTTEST

Spectrum Counting Money

Grade 2

94

Answer Key

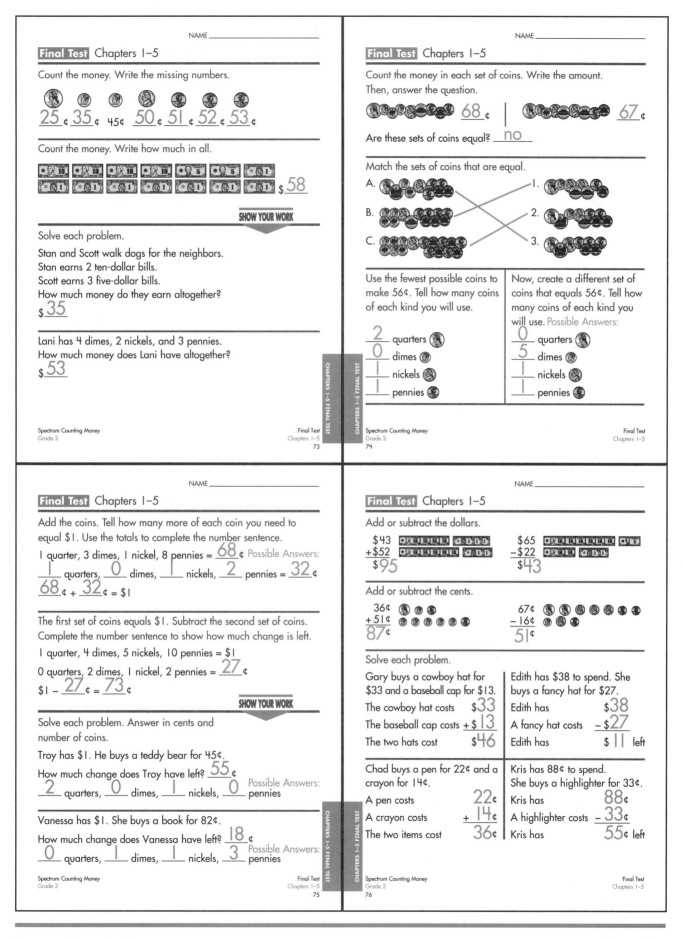

Notes